Inspirations
To Share Through
Our Journey
of Life

by
Linda D. Spence

Table of Contents

Cover photo: *https://www.goodfreephotos.com*

Inspirations
To Share Through Our
Journey of Life
by Linda Spence

Copyright 2011, 2014, 2016 L. Spence

Printed in the United States.

ISBN 978-1-945344-04-6

To purchase an additional copy of this book, please contact me at the following address:

Linda D. Spence
9 County Road 4052
Oxford, Mississippi 38655
https://www.CreateSpace.com/6343817

Inspirations To Share Through Our Journey Of Life

Linda D. Spence

9 County Road 4052
Oxford, Mississippi 38655
1-662-816-1744
SpenceLinda22@yahoo.com

Who Is Linda D. Spence?
Retired after18.5 years; 9/30/1996

Objective:

To be a servant
willing to serve.

Summary of Qualifications:
1/1994 – 9/30/1996 Educational Leadership;
School of Education, University, Mississippi
38677; secretary

8/1991 – 1/1994   Philosophy/Religion
Part-time Secretary; University, Mississippi
38677

1993   Physics Department
Part-time secretary

7/1/1993 – 8/1/1993 TV Representative,
Granada Company, B.M. Hospital, Part-time
Assistant

5/1990 – 8/1991   Mississippi Small Business
Development Center, Senior secretary;
resource coordinator

3/1990 – 5/1990   Psychology Department,
secretary

January – February 1990 Oliver and Sims
Attorneys in Alabama, secretary

10/1985 – 9/1989   Mississippi Law Research Institute, Law Center, senior secretary

5/1984 – 10/1985   Mississippi Law Research Institute, Mississippi-Alabama Sea Grant Program, senior clerk typist

1/1983 – 5/1984   Department of Alumni Affairs, senior secretary

2/1981 – 1/1983   Oxford University, United Methodist Church, secretary (part-time)

1976 – February 1981   Department of Cooperative Education, secretary

Special Skills: trained in the operation of adding machine; Xerox machine, computer terminal, dictating equipment, magnetic typewriter as well as memory typewriter and display writer

Secretarial and business courses completed

Shorthand (90 words a minute; continue to hold Greg Certificate)

Typewriting (78 words a minute; hold certificate)

Speed writing and filing (hold certificate)

Business communications (letter-writing; reports; composition)

English (report writing, composition, and vocabulary)

Other Work Experience:
cashier
sales clerk
receiving clerk
store manager

Education:

Lafayette High School	Graduated May, 1971
University of Mississippi	Sophomore (34 hours)
University of Mississippi	Secretary (18.5 years)

Extracurricular Activities –
Things I Enjoy Doing: Playing
the piano and Singing

Several years worked as a volunteer at Graceland

Volunteer at Golden Years Nursing Homes

Love people; love cheering them up and making them feel better about themselves (I want them to know they are special, because each individual is important.

We each have our talents and special work to accomplish in a lifetime.)

Extracurricular Activities – Volunteer
Present   Volunteer and Full-time Grandmother

2007 – 2009 Volunteer with retired senior volunteer program

2008 - 2008 Volunteer at Graceland – devotion and sing-a-long

2003 - 2007 Volunteer Grandmother

2001 – 2003 Volunteer Chaplain – Baptist Memorial Hospital

1998 – 2000 Volunteer Counselor – Save-A-Life

July – November 2000 Assistant Director, Save-A-Life

Rationale

My Testimony

I just wanted to give God the glory for helping me through all the things that I have experienced in my life.

I wanted to encourage others to know that whatever trials and tribulations we go through in life. God will see us through. He will use every experience to let others know that they can overcome any obstacles that have been a stumbling block in their lives.

Acknowledgement

I, Linda Spence, would like to acknowledge the following persons for helping me complete the book:

Church Family Members

Prayer Groups

Family and Close Friends

Inspirational Writers

Preface

My heart rejoices, and I'm thankful too, that I could share this book with you. This book is truly a "GIFT OF LOVE". All of these poems are woven from words gathered from everywhere.

This is a partnership of three – God first, then you, and last of all me. I am not an author writing for fame; seeking new laurels or praise for my name. I am only a worker employed by the Lord. Great is my gladness and rich is my reward if I can just spread the wonderful story that GOD is the answer to eternal glory.

Only the people who read these poems can help me reach more hearts and homes. We will be sharing new hope, comfort, and cheer. We will be telling sad hearts that there is nothing to fear. What greater joy could there be than to share the love of God and the power of prayer? May GOD's love and His joy flow around this troubled world. May you and I together help to make love and joy realities. This is the wish and the prayer of Linda D. Spence. Sharing the love of God with others really makes this the reason for writing this book.

Dedication

This book is dedicated to my dear friends and family.

Also I would like to dedicate this book to everyone who has come into my life to inspire me to publish this book for the glory of God.

"Without Him I would be nothing for
He touched me."
Philippians 4:13

"For by grace are ye saved through faith, and that not of yourselves; it is the gift of God."
Ephesians 2:8

"I am the vine, and you are the branches. Those who remain in me, and I in them, will bear much fruit, for you can do nothing without me."
(John 15:5)

Introduction

All of the experiences in my life can help others. My love goes to all of those who have shared and laughed with me on this journey called life.

Now I just want to say ... I pray with all my heart ... that "I will meet you there ... in that wonderful place called Heaven ... someday."

God bless each and every one that has helped me along this wonderful journey of life and helped me to share my love for Jesus everywhere I go and have inspired me to become more like Jesus every day of my life.

A very special thank you to my precious family and friends, and everyone who God has placed in my life to encourage me when I was down, and picked me up and gave me courage to carry on... just when I needed it most!

Poetry (acronyms) of

Linda Spence

You Are Very Special –
There's No One Just Like You!

In all the world there's no one like you.

Since the beginning of time, there has never been another person like you.

No one has your smile. No one has your eyes, nose, hair, hands, voice. You are very special.

No one can be found who has your handwriting.

No one anywhere has your tastes for food, clothing, music, or art. No one sees things just as you do.

In all the time there's been no one who laughs like you; no one who cries like you. What makes you laugh and cry will never produce identical laughter and tears from anyone else, ever.

You are the only one in all creation who has this set of abilities. Oh, there will always be someone who will be better at one of the things you are good at, but no one in the universe can reach the quality of your combination of talents, ideas, abilities, and feelings.

Like a room full of musical instruments, some may excel alone, but none can match the symphony. Through all of eternity, no one will ever look, talk, walk, think, or do like you.

You are very special, and I'm beginning to realize it's no accident that we are special. We are beginning to see that God made us special for a purpose.

He must have a job for us that no one else can do as well as we can. Out of all the billions of applicants, only one is qualified, only one has the right combination of what it takes.

That one is you, because you are very special. There is no one just like you!

If I Could Choose My Own Mother

by

Suzanne Spence Potts

If I could choose my own Mother,
I still would choose you...

'Cause no one knows me like you just the way
you always do.
With a loving, caring heart and a very opened
mind, of all the mothers in the world, you are
the only one for me.
No one cares for me like you,
or loves just like you do.

So on this Mother's Day –
just sit back and say:
"At least I know one thing –
I have taught my child to pray."

This day should be a pleasurable one for you.

You know I can pray!!
Happy Mother's Day,
Linda!!!!!

From your loving daughter,
Suzanne Spence
(*Suzanne Spence, 5/5/94*)

Reflections

by Linda Spence

Mission

We the members are being taught in this ministry to know what our spiritual gifts and talents, and resources are to be used for the building up of the Kingdom of God.

Sending us out to minister to people of every race, age, or status with the same love and kindness which we ourselves have received from Jesus Christ.

Freely receive. Freely give.

Vision

- To see people come into the knowledge of a saving relationship with Jesus Christ
- To love God and share His love and knowledge (the word) with others who don't know how much God loves everyone

(Romans 8:1 - There is therefore now no condemnation for those who are in Christ Jesus)

- Creating and keeping a cycle of love to God and to all mankind

Poetry

A Special Recognition

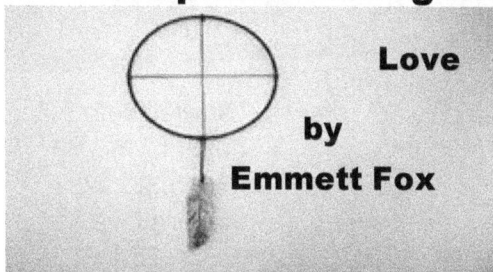

Love

by

Emmett Fox

There is no difficulty that enough love will not conquer;

No disease that enough love will not heal;

No door that enough love will not open;

No Gulf that enough love will not bridge;

No wall that enough love will not throw down;

No sin that enough love will not redeem.

It makes no difference how deeply seated the trouble,

How hopeless the outlook,

How muddled the tangle,

How great the mistake;

A sufficient realization of love will dissolve it all...

If only you could love enough,
you would be the happiest
and most powerful being in the world.

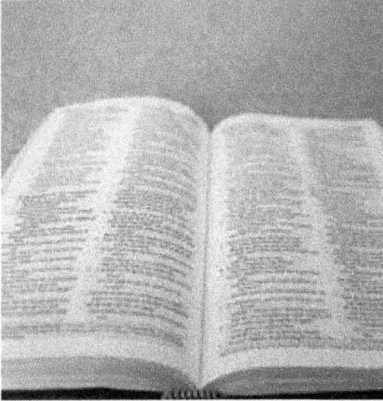

"Now abideth faith,
hope, love – But
the greatest of
these is love."
1 Cor. 13:13

Scriptural

Readings:

Wisdom

A new heart...a new life...another chance to make a difference in this world

Jesus Christ died for all of us.

If you do not know for sure that you have asked Jesus to come into your heart and accepted him as your savior and Lord of your life, please do it now, before it is too late.

All you have to do is ask, believing. You shall receive.

God bless each and every one of you.
Jesus loves you and I do too.

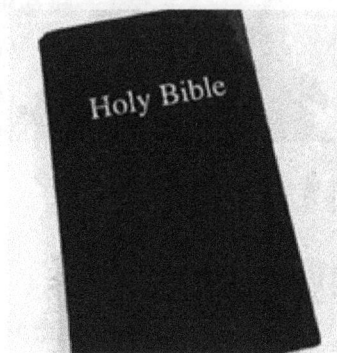

Freedom

(II Chronicles 7:14 – *If my people, who are called by my name, will humble themselves, and repent and turn from their wicked ways...I will hear from Heaven and heal their land.***)**

Go to someone that you trust, and that you know is a Christian. Talk to them and confess every sin that you have committed. Bring it to the light, so that you can be released and be forgiven of all of your sins.

All sins must be brought to the light before we can be healed.

Then pray with them from the bottom of your heart.

The word says where two people join together and pray, sincerely and humbly, He will forgive and heal, and you will become a new creature, and have a new heart and a new life in Jesus Christ.

Ask to be filled with the Holy Spirit, every day to empower you to live the pure and Holy life that Jesus Christ wants you to live. You cannot do it on your own, no matter how hard you try. It takes the Holy Spirit working in you at all times. But it is possible because of Jesus Christ dying on the cross for you and shedding His blood for everyone.

We must get sincere. Get ready - for Jesus is coming back, and we must get forgiven and purified, so that we will be ready for His coming.

Thank God for grace, for mercy, for His unconditional love with His people. Let it be completed. Let's get going.

Restoration

Hungry...and filled with the Holy Spirit...We have the answer to every problem we have or ever will have.

Come on people, The Trinity: God and Jesus, and the Holy Spirit - is waiting on us

Let's go...go...go.

Time is running out. I want to see everyone in Heaven. God knows we are not ready for Him to come. That is why He is waiting to send Jesus Christ back to get us.

Sunrise

God wants everyone to go to Heaven. But, we have to do our part. We are a team. We are Christians. We must stand up and fight for what is right.

Forgive those people who hurt you. No matter what they say back to you, God will take care of the rest. Believe you, me...I have been there and done that...

Renewal

I want revival. I want renewal. I want people to love themselves, and love all people.

Only with God's love in our hearts can we do this.

Come on army, let's get on God's side and with His Holy spirit do our part. He promises in His Word He will do the rest.

We will see things happening all around us. We will see change in our families, our children, our homes, our whole world, the United States of America.

We do want change, but until we get on God's team, and go for it, it will never happen. Let's be positive for a change.

Let's make a difference in ourselves, in our families, in our work. Most of all in our minds.

What you think is what you are! Are you positive? Are you negative? Whose side are you on – God's or the Devil?

I want to be positive, not negative. Every time I think or say a negative, I turn it around to positive. Every time I hear a negative; I turn it around with a positive response. It takes practice. But we can do it with God's help.

Please, come on. Let's go ye into all the
world.

Revival

Pray. Preach. Teach the good news.

Jesus saves. There is still hope. God is not through with us yet. Time is running out. God wants to bless us. Let's let Him do it by doing everything His way – not our way.

Revival must come before it is too late. God is showing mercy and grace on us right now. Let's be in the army of God and get things done. We can do all things through Christ who strengthens us. That is a promise from God's own word.

Let's stand on it. Let's proclaim it. Let's live it. It will work!

We do have the answer. We must stop sinning and trust in the Lord with all of our hearts, and lean not on our own understanding...

God is still in control. Americans, let's go. We are on the

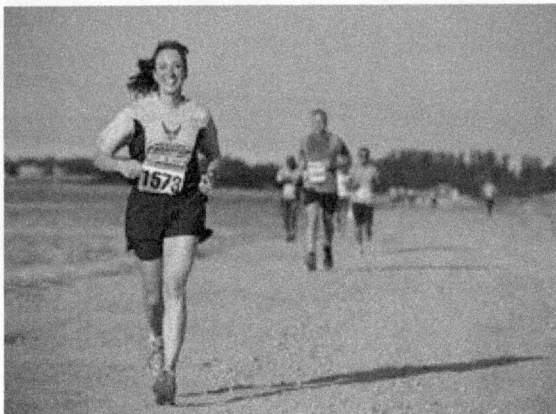

right track.

Let's finish the race. Keep the faith. Do not faint. God still loves us. He has never left us. We are His chosen people.

A Story of My Life

"Precious Memories"

In a very small house, two little girls were born, just ten minutes apart. Linda was born first and, then secondly, but not least, Glenda.

At the time of our birth my family already consisted of our oldest sister Shirley, who was about five years older. Next was our sister Barbara. Barbara was 18 months older than we, the twins, Linda Lou Davis (me) and Glenda Sue Davis (my twin).

Barbara, being only 18 months older always seemed to try to be the boss of all the children. When Mother wasn't around, Barbara stepped in and was the mother image.

We girls loved our one and only brother, Raymond Lynn Davis. He was better known as Bubby. Of course we, the girls, spoiled him rotten.

At the age of six weeks we, the twins Linda and Glenda, rode with our heads on a pillow next to our Mother, from Mississippi to Chicago. We lived in Chicago while my father worked for a trucking business - moving furniture.

Our father got killed in 1956 in a car accident. We were about four years old when our father got killed. We still remember the night the police came to the door and told us of the horrible accident. Our Grandmother Davis was living with us at the time in

Chicago.

After our father died in 1956, we moved back to Lafayette County to be close to my mother's family. My mother did not know how she was going to handle this tragedy, but with the Lord guiding her, she was able to raise us.

We had many happy times in spite of the bad. God does provide. During the year of 1958-1959, I went to Oxford Elementary School. Glenda and I failed the first grade and had to take it over.

Because of the tragedy in our lives, we felt that it had an influence in our ability to learn. In 1960-61 before starting our second grade, we moved to the Lawhorn Place in Etta, MS and transferred to Philadelphia School where we attended from our 2nd grade 1960-61 to 1964-65 through the 6th grade. The

Philadelphia School closed.

Also all small schools were closed and all students were sent to larger schools instead of all the small schools around the county. We all had to make that adjustment from the small schools to the large schools, but finally about the 9th grade I caught on and made better grades. Finally, in 1971, I graduated from Lafayette High School despite the difficulties.

A couple of years passed after the death of our father, 1956-1958. My mother met a bachelor Paul White, and fell in love with him.

(Public Domain Photo)

He played the guitar and was a very talented man. From this marriage came two more children: Daisy Venera White and Mrs. Scott Bullard. Both of them have two children: Misty Bullard and Kate Bullard. Daisy was born on April 8th 1960, thirty minutes after the twins' birthday on April 7th being in 1952 opposed to Daisy's birthday April 8th in 1960.

We lived on the Lawhorn Place at the time. On July 22, 1967, Alice Fay White was born. She was a surprise baby or a "change of life baby". Anyway, my mother became the happy mother of seven beautiful children.

While mother was pregnant with Fay, our stepfather was working for the City of Oxford and grading gravel roads when one day, he pulled up to the Ole Miss Service Station in Oxford to get some air in the grader tire. The tire blew up and hit him in the head.

It was a miracle that he lived. Dr. Bramlett did surgery, releasing the pressure from his brain and rushing him in an ambulance to Memphis for additional medical help. We all know that the Lord was with us during this time and that is why he lived through this accident. We are so thankful that he was a part of our lives from 1958-1994 when he passed away after a period of sickness with cancer.

During most of our growing up years, we lived on the Lawhorn Place and had lots of fun. We had a barn and milked cows. The cows were named after the children, and we rode the bus to school every day. There was a creek behind the barn and we had a lot of fun wading bare-footed.

We went to church at Cambridge United Methodist Church. I can remember one time when we were going to a revival at Cambridge and it was muddy. We got stuck in the ditch while Shirley, the oldest child, was driving the car to church. We didn't know if it was closer to our home or to the church, so we all walked to church and got someone to help us get our car out of the ditch so we could get back home.

We enjoyed living and growing up on the Lawhorn Place. One time when Glenda and I went to bed; we had a pillow fight. Paul, our step-father, came in our room and spanked us. We never did that again.

Several years passed before we moved to the Walker-Down's Place. I lived with my family on the Walker-Down's Place until I married Arlin Curtis Spence on February 6, 1970. I was 17 years old and Arlin was 24.

I can remember that Alice Fay White and Stevie Steele, were only 2 years old when Arlin and I married. We were married at Bro. and Mrs. E. A. Autry's home in Hickory Flat, MS. Mrs. Lola Autry played the piano. About 15 family members were present. Glenda Sue Davis and Gerald Steele were our Best Man and Maid of Honor. It was on Friday Night, February 6, 1970. Brenda Spence Steele made my wedding dress and vail. It was beautiful. We were married February 6, 1970, and Arlin left for Korea on February 26.

I lived with my father-in-law and mother-in-law, Curtis and Loree Spence, while Arlin was gone. They became my real parents. I loved them dearly. I finished high school while Arlin was in Korea. I remember the Principal, Mr. Brewer, took five points off all of my grades because it was in the Oxford Eagle Newspaper that we were married. I took off the day Arlin left to take him to the Memphis, Tennessee airport.

After Arlin got back from Korea, we bought a trailer and completely remodeled it. It looked real nice.

Arlin bought a piano for me before we moved to town in 1976. I was so proud of it. The trailer was very small, but we made room for the piano in the living room. Mr. and Mrs. Patton came over and listened to me play the piano. The piano was great. I had always wanted one. When we moved to town behind the hospital, I had the piano in the first house that we owned.

I won't ever forget when some people from Cambridge Church, my home church, called me and asked me to come back to Cambridge Church to play for the first Sunday night service and they paid me $5 for playing. It made me feel so good.

I was playing the piano for Graceland and Golden Years at the time. It was the same song book that we used at Graceland and I knew most of the songs. I played for Graceland quite some time and I dearly loved playing for the nursing homes and churches.

Because of the tragedies in my life of the past, I have had many fears and not very much confidence in myself or my talents until I met Arlin. I really fell in love with Arlin. It was like he took the place of my father and his love.

I felt I had not really lived until I met Arlin. I worshiped the ground he walked on and really and truly, he became my God. I thought he could do no wrong. I finished high school while he was overseas for 13 months. I lived with Arlin's parents, Curtis and Loree Spence, while Arlin was in Korea. I really enjoyed living with my husband's parents. I felt that Mr. Spence was like my father, since I had not had a father that I could remember because my father died when I was only 4 years old. He, Mr. Spence, helped me so much with my ability to learn how to play the piano.

We went to Bay Springs Baptist Church. He led the singing while I played the piano. It was such joy and he encouraged me so much.

When Arlin got back from Korea, we bought a trailer and lived below his parents for several years. A spring was just below our trailer and we were able to drink spring water. It was the best water I had ever had to drink.

In 1976, we bought a house in town behind the hospital. Arlin worked for the City of Oxford Electric Department. I worked for Rebel Press at first when we married. In 1976, I started working for the University of Mississippi. I worked for the University from 1976 to 1996 with a few breaks between service.

Arlin and I were married for 10 years before we became the happy parents of Arlinda Suzanne Spence Potts who has brought so very much happiness into our lives. I feel she is an angel from above. I must say that having a child after being married 10 years, was quite a change though. Arlin and I both had to change, buckle down, and we were not able to do just as we pleased. Nor were we able to go when we both got ready. As all parents know, life changes when you have a little one.

When our one and only brother got married, Raymond Lynn Davis, he married a girl named Glenda Ruth Davis – almost with the same name as my twin sister's name, Glenda Sue Davis. When Glenda and Bubby were married, they asked me to play the piano for them. I was so excited. It was hard to believe that they wanted me to play the piano. I didn't think I was good enough, but for them to ask me to do it…I was very excited and happy that they thought that I could do it.

I picked out some beautiful songs that I thought I could play. I asked Marilyn Davis, my first cousin's wife, to come over to my house and teach me how to do "Here Comes the Bride". I was so excited. I had never played for a wedding before. It turned out to be a beautiful wedding and I had people come up to me and ask me how I could play so well.

I am happy that I was able to play for their wedding.

On March 15, 1980, Arlinda Suzanne Spence was born to the proud parents of Arlin and Linda Spence. On April 8, 1980, Raymond and Glenda became the proud parents of Josh Davis. On July 23, 1980 Daisy and Scott Bullard became the proud parents of Misty Bullard. Three babies were born in five months. Linda Spence, Glenda Ruth Davis and Daisy Bullard were all pregnant at the same time.

I have always said, be ye ware, Caesar in literature. (The ides of March) When Suzanne was born, I had a bad case of depression. It continued over into the third month after her birth. I have had some problems with depression ever since.

For one thing, I have always been jealous of Arlin and Suzanne. I felt that ever since Suzanne was born that Arlin showed more attention to her than to me. When Arlinda Suzanne was born and was three months old, I had to be taken to Memphis for depression.

The doctors didn't know how to treat it. So from 1980-1984 we just had to deal with it. When Suzanne was born, I became what some people would call a religious fanatic.

I had a big unexplainable experience where I believed that the World was coming to an end. I believed it with all my heart. It was as though God placed this on my heart. I was concerned about all my loved ones and their salvation.

The real thing that happened in my life was for the first time in my life I felt the forgiveness of Jesus Christ, in my life. I felt that I had been forgiven for every sin that I had committed. What a great feeling! I had been carrying my burdens for the last

10 years. Finally, I had been forgiven and I now had a wonderful child.

I wanted to start over again with the beautiful child that was just given to us and forget the past. I told Arlin this but it was hard for him to believe. Ever since that time, I have felt the forgiveness of God and have wanted to live a Christian life and walk with Christ every day. I have a deep burden for those that are lost and do not know the forgiveness of Christ.

In 1980 I was sent to Memphis and placed in the psychiatric ward for being a religious fanatic. I had to see Dr. Beatus, which I didn't really like. In 1984 I had a wonderful doctor, Dr. Melvin Levitch, who I think is a Christian doctor. He and I got along fine. I gave him notes telling him all of my problems. This was kind of like the story of my life.

In 1984 Dr. Levitch put me on Lithobid which is a drug for depression. I have had to go back in the hospital almost every two years 1980, 1982, 1984, 1986, 1989, and 1990 thru 1997). The symptoms in all of these experiences, have always been the concern of the salvation of my family. The other concern was of me being a religious fanatic because of what God had done for me in my life.

In 1987 my husband's mother died. I had found a poem called "Heaven's Grocery Store". We placed it in memory of her in the Intensive Care Unit. Three years later, my husband received that same poem in his birthday card from his stock company. I believe what you send out will come back to you.

See, my husband and daughter have bought

stock in a company. I tell them that my stock is in the Lord Jesus Christ. Arlin's mother was in the Intensive Care Unit for six weeks, so I have much compassion for those that go through similar situations. I sometimes go to the hospital and just talk and visit those that have sick ones.

I have been collecting poems as long as I can remember. I really enjoy doing it. While working for the MS Law Research Institute at the Law School, Brenda and Joan Daniels showed me their book, "Joy In The Morning". That's when I wanted to type it and get it published or copyrighted for them. They let me have it to type for them. With the help of many persons we went to work and we now have it placed in many doctors' and dentists' offices.

At the same time, I thought, "Well I have some of my poems on the computer, I will make a

book for me at the same time for the Glory of God."
We put the two books together and we went to work.
I had help from many people. The poem book is
called "Gleanings From Here, There and
Everywhere".

I found out about a tract company in Indiana.
I have been sharing their poems with as many people
as I can. They have some really good poems. This
company also has the poem "Heaven's Grocery
Store" that was placed in the hospital in memory of
Loree Spence.

One time I asked my daughter, "If you had
one wish and only one wish in all the world, what
would it be?"

"I wish I would get to go to heaven," she said.
"Isn't that great."

Shortly after Suzanne got saved, she wrote in

a little notebook of exactly what songs she wanted sung at her funeral. She also wrote down what clothes to use. She left the notebook "to whomever finds this notebook. This is what I want at my funeral." I found it one day while cleaning the house.

In 1988 my husband's Granny died, six months after his mother died. Granny lived in the Graceland Nursing Home. During that time, I began to play the piano and when Granny died, I could not stop playing there.

So we began a program. It has been a wonderful experience playing the piano. I love them all at the nursing homes. They are my second family. Bettye Davis and myself had a program we called the "Patient's Program" where they chose the songs they wanted to sing. Bettye played the piano and I helped lead the singing. It was such joy.

In 1989, as I previously stated, while working in the MS Law Research Institute in the Law School, I with the help of many others, worked together and put together a book of poems entitled Gleanings From Here, There, and Everywhere. Also I took Joy In The Morning, the book written by Joan and Brenda Daniels and revised it. We bound it so we could share it with others. We went to the bank and borrowed the money and placed copies of both books in the doctors' and dentists' offices and the Retardation Center. We did this for the Glory of God.

Joan and Brenda got so excited about the "Joy In The Morning" book and how people asked for copies of it. We took copies of poems and placed them in people's rooms that were sick in the hospital.

In 1989 Arlin's Aunt Bessie who was retarded died. When Loree died and Granny died there was no one to go and get Bessie and do for her. So I, Linda, did that for her. It was so much joy. She was such a sweet person.

When Bessie died, this was the first time that Black people and white people at the Retardation Center had ever been involved or felt a part of a funeral. There was love there that cannot be explained. All the people at the Retardation Center said they were amazed. Bessie loved everyone. One of the employees of the Retardation Center wrote a poem in memory of Bessie and I have a copy of it at home.

In 1989 in the middle of the night it came to me to have a Bible Balloon Birthday Party at both of the nursing homes. I had played and visited both of the nursing homes and loved many of the patients in both of them. I called both nursing homes and set it up. We had it at the Golden Years facility on Tuesday, and at Graceland on Wednesday of the same week. It was such joy. This was a joy that I can't explain.

The patients participated and everything went smoothly. We did all of this for the Glory of God and nothing else. We had ministers to come and say the prayer and we all gathered together on the outside and sent the balloons up into the air. It was beautiful and the Oxford Eagle Newspaper came and put it in the Oxford Eagle.

Then we had a revival in September of 1989, at North Oxford Baptist Church. We had a great time. The night, Suzanne was saved. Suzanne and I had called Brenda and Joan's mother and told her to come and bring the van that she had for Brenda and Joan to ride in and we would come to the Nursing

Home and get them that night so they could all come. Needless to say, I did not know, but thank goodness, the van was automatic. I could not have driven a straight shift. I was so nervous that the van was not easy to drive. Thank goodness we all made it there that night and people of the church helped us inside the church. But I feel that God knew how much I wanted Brenda and Joan to get to go to our church and He showed His love by Suzanne getting saved. Arlinda Suzanne Spence was saved on Tuesday, September 20, 1989.

On Friday night of the revival we packed. After the revival was over on Saturday, we left Oxford going to Alabama. I felt the Lord leading me to be baptized. We were in Alabama on Saturday and I went to the preacher there and asked him if he would baptize me on Sunday morning after the 11:00

service.

We should have been on our way back to Oxford, but I didn't care. I had a burden to be baptized. He said he would do it. So I took my clothes and I was baptized in the Martin Lake in Alabama. The sermon that Bro. Allen preached was about the people in the Old Testament and how they gathered together and prayed and worshipped for 8 days and nights without stopping.

I thought… "What a wonderful thing to do and I wish we would do that too." I will not forget the sermon…They did not go to work, nor do anything but worship. They meant business with the Lord.

On Tuesday, September 20, Arlinda Suzanne Spence was saved and Arlin's mother's birthday was September 19, and his sister's birthday is September

19 and Arlin's mother died on September 19, 1987.

I thought Suzanne might accept the Lord during Bible school during the summer when she and I went and I taught, but the Lord knew that she was not ready then. I had a wonderful time teaching that summer in Bible school. I shall never forget it. I was the assistant teacher to Phyllis Clark, who sat by me in church.

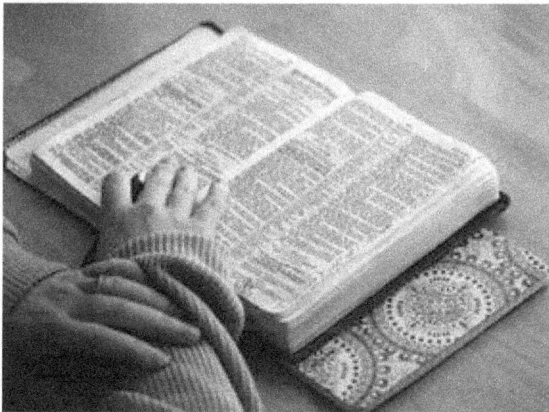

One Sunday morning Phyllis and I were sitting together in church, and I asked her to help with the Bible school and there she was new in the church and was just waiting for someone to ask her. I wanted someone to help me. It was amazing how the Lord put us together. We talk about that still today. We had such a wonderful time during Bible school.

I felt the Lord calling me to give my testimony to those children. I did and I couldn't help but cry. The children seemed to enjoy listening to my testimony. Suzanne wanted to be in our class, but I guess, it wasn't meant to be that Suzanne should be in our class.

Afterward, we were in the process of deciding on whether or not to move to Alabama and work for Arlin's sister and brother-in-law. Arlin had worked for the City of Oxford for 17 years and was very unhappy with the new person in charge at the City. He did not feel that he could keep on working there.

Well, not many weeks after that, I was in the Memphis hospital with depression again because of all the pressures of moving to Alabama and I did not feel that was the real thing for us to do. So I told Arlin "Whatever he decided, I would support him."

We moved to Alabama and lived for four months. Arlin and Suzanne had to do all the moving because I was in the hospital. Dr. Levitch was my doctor, and by the time I got out of the hospital, I was so drugged up that I could not work. Then I had to find a doctor in Alabama to help me get off the medication.

During this time, I went and found the

nursing home there and I got to meet and love those people there who were lonely. I sang with them and played games with them and spent about half of my days off with them. I enjoyed it so much and I can see how God let me be used even when I didn't know it. They helped me so much when I needed help too.

Just one month before we moved back to Oxford, MS I found a joy working in an attorney's office which I dearly loved. The girl I worked with was just delightful. We realized that Alabama was not the place for us so in four months, we started trying to find a way to move back to Oxford.

I got on the telephone one day and I called Deborah Smith and asked her if there was a position in the Accounting Office. I had asked Deborah over and over again before in the 14 years that I worked for the University and she had always said "NO".

For the First Time...Just When We Needed It Most...Deborah said, "Yes, there is a position in the Accounting Office".

I told Arlin to call Mr. Dowdy that night and tell him that he was interested. I know without a shadow of a doubt that God from Heaven sent that job to my husband, Arlin. So we got to move back to Oxford. We may not know, but God has a purpose in all that happens to us in our lives. God can make the best out of the times that we think are the worst.

On March 3, 1990, I came back to Oxford, MS alone while Arlin and Suzanne stayed in Alabama. I found a job in the Psychology Department at the University of MS. I worked in the Psychology Dept. from March to May, 1990. I did not think the patients were being treated right because the students did not take their patients serious enough.

They, the students, didn't have the compassion that I felt they needed to show towards the patients. I had been a patient in a different situation, and on May 1, 1990, I transferred to the MS Small Business Development Center as Senior Secretary. I had worked for the University of MS for 14 years except for a break in service once or twice. I worked at the MS Small Business Development Center from May until October, 1990. In October, 1990, I had a spell with a chemical imbalance (Bi-Polar) and left the office one day on Thursday, and no one knew where I was.

I went to a friend of mine, Ms. Mary Shepherd's in Water Valley. This was not the first time I had done things like this. I finally called and told Arlin and Suzanne where I was and I was admitted to the Oxford Hospital. Dr. Randle was my doctor. I stayed in the Oxford Hospital a couple of days and then I was sent to the Jackson Medical Hospital.

Dr. Randle let me visit other patients while I was in the Oxford Hospital. To talk to me, you wouldn't think there was anything wrong with me. I was just upset with my family and on fire for the Lord.

I got to Jackson and my doctor was Dr. Richardson. They were amazed with my faith and strong belief and the love of God. I was in the hospital for 4 weeks and Dr. Richardson got my chemical imbalance back in order. So I went back to work at Ole Miss as soon as I was told to do so by my doctor.

I wrote to the Chancellor Turner about my

stay in the hospital in Jackson and I told him that there was one ingredient that was missing in the Ward. That was love. They also did not let us share poems or talk too much about religion. That was a deep concern of mine.

On June 5, 6, and 7th I got to go to Starkville, MS with the MS Small Business Development Center to our regular quarterly conference. I really had a great time. Our bus driver was a guy that knew some people. One in particular was Suzanne Buckner. I had worked with her in Bible school. That was great to know. I also met some very nice people and I took some real nice pictures.

As soon as I got back to Oxford from the Starkville trip, our daughter, (Arlinda Suzanne) was sick all night Monday night and on Tuesday of that week. We took her to the doctor (Tom Glasgow).

and he and Dr. Harris said we needed to take her by ambulance to Memphis to LeBonheur. She was diagnosed a diabetic. She was a very sick girl. Her sugar was up to 600 and Suzanne and myself had to go in the ambulance. Arlin came on behind us. The ambulance driver was a lady and the EMT was Ron Smith. Suzanne really liked him.

Just the other day we went back to the hospital in Oxford and gave them all some small gifts for all that they had done for us. Gay White put the needle in Suzanne's arm to start the IV and a nurse named Kelly was very nice to us. We sent the LeBonheur doctors and nurses something too. That was a lot of fun. We were so very thankful that Suzanne did not go into a coma or get any worse than she did. Suzanne was so very brave through the whole thing. We are very proud of her.

I worked for the MS Small Business Development Center for a while. I feel that there was a purpose for me working there, I just don't understand it all right now. I am very thankful for the opportunity of working with Grace Gunter and Norma White and Jeff Terry and Uric and Suzie. They have been very nice to me. I am thankful that God let me work with someone by the name of Grace. She is a very nice person and her personality fits her name.

I was employed with the University of MS for 18 and one-half years. I dearly loved working for the University. I retired on September 30, 1996 and was able to receive disability because of my Bi-Polar medical condition. I think we have a lot to be thankful for with the University in Oxford, MS. I have met many wonderful people and it has been a joy to work for Ole Miss. I hope things get better and the pay scale will get better for all concerned.

During the first of July, I saw a request for a poem in the *Sunshine Magazine* asking for submissions. The poem which was to be written was to be entitled "What Would You Do If Jesus Came To Your House Today?" I sent some of my poems along with the poem she requested, to the lady from Keysville, VA. Her name is Elsie Forehand. This lady is 84 years old with the most beautiful handwriting. She received 72 letters and chose my letter out of 3-4 letters. The poems she received were from 29 different states.

Her husband is a preacher and has been for 60 years. He has committed his life to establishing churches and then moving on. What a beautiful story. This lady said that she was old and her health was bad. I encouraged her to please write those 72 people back even if it took one letter a day...Just think 72 letters and 29 different states. It sounds like the Lord Himself has opened up her doors of her house and given her the ability to write to 72 different people and 29 different states. Isn't that a great ministry...just for one person? Sounds great to me. I hope she will do just that and have a ministry just like her husband has in churches. She has a ministry in her home too. I look forward to hearing from her soon. I sent Elsie Forehand a copy of books Gleanings From Here, There and Everywhere and also Joy In The Morning.

I gave Mr. Samuels in the University Publications Center on campus a copy of "Gleanings and Joy" for him to read and give back to me. I hope he will enjoy them.

God blesses me with so many wonderful opportunities and blessings every day. God walks and talks with me and as long as I let Him, God will guide my every footstep. I hope and pray that whoever reads this story will be blessed and be able to see the power of God and what God can do for each of us each and every day when we yield and let Him take control of our lives.

This I hope you will do. God loves us so very much. We must love God with all our heart, soul, and mind and love our neighbors as ourselves.

God Bless and Keep You Until We Meet Again...If not in person, may it be in Heaven...Some Day.!!!

A Final Thought!

A Message From Linda Spence

Linda's Obituary

To my dear friends:

Some funny things happened to me on the way to heaven.

The first memories I recall were all happy ones. From the beginning, I felt joy, safety and contentment - each a product, I realize, of my loving mother.

Being in a place with my mother was always special. Most of all, it was safe. It was at a place I fondly called home.

Also, my mother and step-father loved me unconditionally. My real Father passed away in a car accident when I was only 4 years old. God had already put into motion, the pursuit of a worthy girl.

I was surrounded by one wonderful brother and five sisters. Sure there were yelling and tugging, but mostly there was laughter.

It seemed that my family preferred to smile, even in

adversity. I recall several events like pillow fights, running out of gas, and playing basketball. My family preferred to "laugh it off" and carry on with the day.

As I grew, it came time to move forward. At the wonderful age of 17, I was married and working for a living. I always had jobs that I loved. I rarely felt as if I was really working. I was getting paid to do exciting and fun things.

Then, after 10 years had passed, at the age of 28, we became the happy parents of a wonderful daughter, Arlinda Suzanne Spence.

I do not know about love at

first sight. For me, it was love at first smile. To this day, my husband's smile melts my heart. For his smile – I would do anything. I loved him dearly.

Yet as the years have passed, my love for him has grown into something that I can't explain.

We loved being together. Each other's presence was enough to give us peace, security and satisfaction. Being together became the place we lovingly called home.

Our home sometimes contained echoes of laughter. You see, when he loved our daughter, Arlinda Suzanne, all was good.

Our home was blessed beyond measures with a job and responsibility of raising, and laughing with our daughter.

Suzanne has grown to be a young woman for whom I have the highest respect. She has faced the opportunities that have come her way with courage and honor. She loves to entertain you. She has the wonderful gift of compassion, and is a friend to everyone she meets.

I am going now to a place that has been prepared for me. There will be laughter there too. We know there will be no tears.

So, I'm expecting fun -

something beyond my wildest imagination – a place I am not worthy to be – a place I have longed to go. It is the place I have lived for, and longing to call my eternal home.

My love goes to all of those who have shared, and laughed with me on this journey called life.

Now I just want to say – I pray with all my heart, that I will meet you there in that wonderful place called Heaven – someday.

God bless each and every one that has helped me along this wonderful journey of life, and helped me to share my love for Jesus everywhere I go, and have inspired me to become more like Jesus every day of my life.

A very special thank you to my precious family and friends; and everyone that God has placed in my life to encourage me when I was down.

You picked me up and gave me courage to carry on, just when I needed it most!

Just remember, this world is not a bed of roses. But, the best is yet to come.

God bless you all.

I send all of my love to everyone.

See you all in Heaven someday.

That is my prayer!
Linda Spence
April 7, 1952 - Present

www.ingramcontent.com/pod-product-compliance
Lightning Source LLC
Chambersburg PA
CBHW021212020426
42331CB00003B/333